Spiritual Travelers
. . . on our own without a map

D1606673

Tony Prewit

Spiritual Travelers . . . on our own without a map
copyright Tony Prewit, 2014 all rights reserved
Published by Ridgeline Press
Silver City, New Mexico, U.S.A.
ISBN 978-0-9854487-6-9

Editing, book design, cover design, and production services by Heidi
Connolly, Harvard Girl Word Services
Cover artwork by Tony Prewit

Acknowledgments

I would like to thank my wife, Patricia Prewit, for the years of assistance in sorting, editing, and proofreading all my work. I thank her most of all for being her and allowing me to continue to be the person she married. I would also like to thank my editor, Heidi Connolly, who helped with the final sculpturing of this book. Her vision, talent, and professional guidance have been invaluable.

Other Books by Tony Prewit

Six-book Series: *Journey in the Mind's Eye of a Poet*
    Journal of Time
    Portals and Passages
    The Book of the Lost and Found or Chasing Rainbows
    Moods of War
    The Source
    Another Day

The Observer

Table of Contents

Prologue

If we are not changing in heart, mind, or body, then we are not traveling far. Change is the journey of life — and even truth can change.

How so?

The truths we discover move with time. Even the stars and galaxies are born and, in time, die out. If the universe is forever changing, can we then infer that our world is forever changing, too, and that our truths change as well?

Whether we might choose to transform or not, change is a part of our being; the fact of our aging is the certain evidence. For me, the perplexing part here is that even though we are forever changing, we appear to be without a spiritual map to direct us in how to adapt to these changes.

The collection of poems in this book interprets the voices I hear as well as those of the many people I see as we journey together through an ever-changing world.

Part One, *Travelers*, explores our spiritual quests as well as our failures or successes in those quests — though we may not recognize them as such until time has passed.

Part Two, *Fado*, or Longings, explores our tendency to want certain things to be true, and our unwillingness to accept them when they are not. I define "longing" as an unattainable want. In my opinion, we all tend to exert our will, faith, and energy in order to ensure that what we want will manifest in our lives. Yet, regardless of our efforts — physical, mental, emotional, and/or spiritual — there will always be times when the events we want to happen simply do not. When such times occur, our wants and desires and needs — like love, survival, justice, freedom, and healing—appear crucial. Yet, it is clear that the ability to justify or defend these desires has no bearing on whether or not their outcome will manifest, and/or manifest in the way we want.

The concept of longing first came to my attention when I learned about the Portugese music called *fado*. *Fado* is characterized by mournful tunes and lyrics and is often infused with a kind of melancholy. Loosely translated, the word *saudade* means "longing." Although I can only speak from my own Americanized view of this experience of *fado* and the depths of the longing it describes, I offer my insights here into what happens when our desired outcomes do not occur, given the indisputable fact that eventually we all fall victim to such longings.

Part Three, *The Priest in Us*, contemplates my belief that we all hold the capacity to be our own guides, both worldly and spiritual, in life. This section also explores my belief that we are not required to follow or believe in any religion or faith that does not suit us. After all, is not God big enough to accommodate all our beliefs and guide each of us through life? Is not the fact that we all have similar inner traits evidence of a common ground in our priesthoods? And, finally, is not this common ground the space God gives us for the capacity to be the true priests of our own lives?

I invite you to explore such questions with me.

Part One: Travelers

Rain Clouds and Life

the rain clouds came quick
though i saw them from a distance
i ran for cover as always
out of breath i leaned against
a wood rail inside an
abandoned barn

the rain passed
the sun came out
i felt refreshed and renewed
i quickly forgot about the
drenching i got when the day
turned out fine.

Where Does Time Go

clouds are like dreams
they float they change
they are fantasy they are real
clouds are truth and serenity

i stare upward and disappear
somewhere inside myself
space with no boundaries
time with no measure

if i could exist without space
    and time
and remember them as they
    once were
my questions would be

    — what is space and
    where does time go.

New Haiku Rules

1.
contemplating
wisdom
is a risk worth
taking.

2.
many miracles
begin small
and grow
like seeds.

3.
the more money
i need the less
i become.

4.
the greater my
debt
the greater
my
need.

5.
beliefs are
greatly
challenged
when
compromise
is the only
way

—perhaps the
problem here
is our perspective.

Spiritual Mutt

my spiritual beliefs
are a mix of
many

i am not a purebred of
any one belief and am
not loyal to only one
or to any belief
entirely.

Moon One

silent moon
no sound

you beckon
me to listen

i hear the
night breeze

nocturnal animals
busy about their tasks

    i wake

moonlight not
of its own

but borrowed
from the sun

reflections and shadows
in motion

while a pair of eyes in
darkness stare at me

    i see

full moon shine on
inspire me

speak to me of
revelations

whatever or whoever
created this

and created me
i thank you

i awe.

Moon Two

my friend
moon
judge me
not
let me
sit
under your
light
and confess
secrets
i know you
will
keep.

Moon Three

the moon will not
help with rent
or feed me if i am
starving

the moon does not
visit me when
i am ill or in
need

rather it is i who must
seek the moon
and i who must
speak first

yet the moon is still a
friend on whom
i can count
when silence and
light are what i
need.

Moon Four

moon light
moon bright
you are full tonight
i have you in my sight

seduce me to wander awhile
through the miles and miles
of my *inner-magination*

will you guide me tonight
till the sun rises and
dawn wakens and lifts
my soul to new
heights.

Hu-man Clips

    1.
what is the spirit made of

hu-mans i suppose

is there an answer
that will satisfy

hu meaning of God
man meaning
of earth

     what else could it mean.

    2.
i hu-man am in conflict
with my own being
as if God and earth
mix not

we war with ourselves as
if all it takes is one more
death to find the peace
we seek

the more powerful we
become the more
intolerant we
grow

     what else could it mean.

3.

is the *man* part of me
meant to bow to the *hu* part of me
are we to allow our souls to seek after
the Spirit who made us
hu-man
     – soul and Spirit
     – earth and God

     what else could it mean.

Jesus the Hu-man

what more could i ask of you
than your life

you stood as a giant among
hu-mans

they took your body but not
your voice

jesus the lesser no deity in
him do i esteem

far greater is he to me as
hu-man

as a God he would have
failed

but as a hu-man his words
inspire me

to become better at being
hu-man

what more could i ask
of anyone than that.

Eulogy to David

1.
david had diabetes

he was a kind man
an honest man

he was intellectually gifted
a talented musician

he had seven children and
a wife who all loved him

david did not care for
himself much

nor did he take precautions
with his diet

he died at fifty-two and the last
few years were misery

he slowly lost his eyesight
and legs and a few fingers

he gained an enormous
amount of weight

he could have slowed his death
and enjoyed more quality of life

i mourn his death and am relieved he did not
put his family through more agony

the tragedy is it did not have to be this way
—not even close.

    2.
goodbye my friend and may heaven
be better for you than earth was

may your wife and children be restored of
what you took from them
how you leaned on them.

      the mystery of david is why he chose
      this path and why he defended it.

Right Brain Rambler

at eighty-one i realize i
mostly live in my right brain
though foggy it is

the peace i feel is different
from when i lived in my left brain
everything had to add up

i prefer my left but my right
allows me dreams

i was unaware when i switched from
my left brain to my right

but now at eighty-one i take the time to
inform you about its importance

though i do switch back and forth
anxiety rules when i try too much

i never have control in the switching
it is a see-saw

it is called aging—

when thinking about tomorrow
becomes a chore

when living in the past leads us to believe
we will last forever

when we are constantly frustrated and confused
as to the workings of our brain

when the rational expands beyond any known
definition

when the home we dream of is within reach
when we barely hear those around us

and when time has no meaning
our final phase has begun

> *past memories our rock*
> *today's memories forever lost*
> *unaware we are that our days have become*
> *an opiate for us as a guide through*

> > *yours truly —*
> > *right brain rambler signing off.*

The Six

they are real and
imaginary
—they are called "the six"

referring to six men i remember from
bible studies i attended before work
through the years

the six embody conservative
evangelical christianity

arrogant dominating
self-righteous with
hardly any be-
havioral traits
that remind
me of
christ

i was totally unaware of my
obsession with the six
until one day a friend
told me that i bring
them up in con-
versation often
when referring
to my past
disgusts

it is an out-of-body experience
when i talk about them be-
cause i do not remember
mentioning them at all
it is as if they have
ruined my ob-
jectivity on
the subject.

The Slap Was Hard

slaps are hard
lights are blinding
both eyes swollen shut
bruises and cuts
too many to count

pain so unbearable
he slips into
a space of no return

questions now useless
the men administering torture
are unaware

to them the prisoner suffering greatly
should breakdown at any moment
tell them everything they want to hear

but he was in a place of bliss
incoherent the pain hot
like ice

— stuck in time and space
where the existence of pain
has no present no past
no future

his right brain shut off the pain
while his torturers still unaware
agitated in their left brains

but the mystery was not new to the master interrogator
who had encountered it before
he would remind the others

  — too much pain
  too quick

  go slow
  or we will lose him.

Wrong

those who describe
their worship as the only way
to worship God and the only way
God accepts worship
— are wrong.

This Is Big News

to see God on earth
is experienced in our value of life
to see God in spirit
is experienced in our value of faith.

Jots

1.
is evolution the universe's
way of keeping time

is change a God-created
feature of the universe.

2.
should our view of God and how
to approach God be subject to change.

3.
are we made to evolve and change.

4.
some things have not changed
like the continual cruelty we inflict
upon the earth.

5.
thinking up wisdom in verse is a jot
to the universe.

How It Would Be

if you and i were birds
we would be red-tailed hawks
and i would search the skies for you
till i found you

i would give you
the belly of a snake from
my beak and embrace you
as we held each other
free-falling
toward
earth

and before
we touched land we would
part and turn upward to the sky and
embrace again

then we would make a nest
—together you and i

—*if you and i were*
red-tailed hawks
this is how
it would
be.

Loft

i am secure in my loft above my room as
if in another dimension

i stare down from above the weight of
my world suspended in time

we all need such a loft

without one we would not know life
without weight.

Journey In

each time i *journey in*
the more i know
how little we
know of the
spiritual
realm

i see how great
my needs are

i see that God
has no needs

i see no real
answers

> —so is my *journey in*
> failure or success.

Whom Do You Seek

i think we are not like God at all . . . i think God
has not the need or want to make any creation in the same
form

i am glad we are not in the image of God for it would
disappoint me to know we were as God.

Presence of Light One

with eyes closed
i wait for a stillness
inside me to arise

a light appears and
wraps itself around
me engulfing me

no voice has the light
no form has the light
it is only light

> *i fear this*
> *reality has*
> *consequence*
> *because i want*
> *to proclaim*
> *it is from*
> *God.*

Presence of Light Two

do not pass me by
light my dark place

my prayer has come
to a dead end

is it here You are
supposed to be

are you the One
i seek

why this light with
no answer

if i dare believe in
You how i conceive of You

will my belief fail as it has
a thousand times

> *the day waits not for me*
> *to find a path through it*
>
> *no earthly or spiritual*
> *entity cares about my dilemma.*

Altars of Lesser Gods

1.
altars of the lesser gods filled with
books and rules . . . icons of gold and silver
. . . marble and wood

altar of the greater God in us
needs not books and icons. . .
gold and silver. . . marble and wood.

2.
a light came to me
humbling me
accepting me

not satisfied i built an
altar and bowed to it

still unsatisfied i wrote a book
and saw myself as superior to those who
believed not as i

— believing that the light had
shone on me alone.

3.
i am now servant to a lesser god

why was i dissatisfied with a God
with no walls altars or penned words.

When in Rome

he shared with me
the beauty and wisdom
of his father a pastor of
a pentecostal church

he grieved over his father's
two heart attacks
over three months' time

he told me how his father
can recite scripture by rote
even with dementia

he told me he had fears of dying
but he knows his father is ready

he told me his father is a light
to him in living and in dying

he said all is in God's hand
and he is glad he is a christian

i listened intently and agreed
with every word

he is my barber my friend though
i have not been a christian for a while
i am at peace and can contribute to
such conversations and situations
without conflict or threat

     — when in rome.

Four Paradoxes

paradox one

we are a paradox unto ourselves
preaching God's safety as tragedy
follows

paradox two

we are a paradox unto ourselves
doing the power of our God while
we war for peace

paradox three

mystery of life you have a hold on me
though i have no answer
i believe no one else
has either

why is the peace in me knowing
that we are in it together and
that no one has the single
answer

paradox four

why do paradoxes make truths
mysterious.

Refraction of Thought

1.
rainbows
sunlight

nature
refracting
light

truth
requiring
inquiry.

2.
moisture
and light
creating
colors

and me
equating
them to my
soul.

3.
is a friend
someone who
lifts us up
from
despair

if so
this
rainbow
is a friend

colors and
light
lifting my
soul.

Ocotillo

ocotillo flower
rich red
blooms
a
hummingbird
hoovers
around
it

i
forget
my
problem
as i
watch
the scene
unfold

the
hummingbird
jabs
accurately
into the
center of
the rich red
ocotillo
flower

so much
effort
for so little
nectar

or so it
seems

how many
ocotillo flowers
does it
take
to
satiate
a
hummingbird

a cloud
shades the
ocotillo
the hummingbird
disappears

and my
thoughts on
my unsolved
problem
reappear

sounds like
life to me.

Frames, Credit, Need

frame

why *frame* God
    why picture God
why give God a beard
    and arms and legs and
eyes and ears

credit

why give God *credit* for the words in our books
    why give God *credit* for rules and creeds
and doctrines and theologies and thrones

need

what is it we *need* that causes us
    to give God praise
for our own beliefs.

Sense of Truth

is it the number
of people
who belong
to a group
that prove its truth

does a style
or ritual prove
virtue or
righteousness

> i sense we
> have become
> convinced
> our own
> beliefs
> are true
> —based upon
> the immaterial nature
> of facts.

White Raven

1.

white raven
saint from heaven

is there a reason
for your creation

or are you a freak
mutation

rare bird you soar
the skies

white yet full of color
full of wonder

i pause to watch
you in flight

does the creator have
a special purpose for you

or is your color only a cover
to survive

either way
i am touched to the core of my soul
each time i catch sight of you.

2.

lonely am i that day till the white raven whisks
above the rock which i am perched

the white speckled creature
i feel sure will be good company

> *we are the same you and i*
> *rare breeds*
> *i in my poet's clothes am just as rare as you*
> *in your white feathers*

my heart soars with you
as i watch you soar the sky

i grab humility
i want you as my friend.

    3.
white raven
saint from heaven

deep red eyes
spying me out

your shadow above me
merging with mine

fierce but not cruel
surveying the ground

prey is on your mind
as you soar without sound

at my feet lies a snake vertical
upon a rock

as swift as the wind
without a sound
lifting the reptile with
your beak

to the sky you jet
till you disappear like air

stunned by the split-second
motion of the raven

beauty and fear lift as one

the snake
now dinner at your nest

> *— a blessing for me*
> *is a curse for the snake*
> *your appearance on that day.*

Part Two: Fado (Longings)

Introduction

longing for what we cannot have
— circumstances of life denying us
our dreams, wants, and needs

life . . . God . . . why so unfair

youthful love tragedy accidents health money
oppression inequality rewards of toil denied

will the force of longing cause us to journey inside
to find a peace or an anger at having been denied
what we believe is justifiably ours

if longing is the struggle between hope and no hope
can we be at peace with life despite the withholding
of what we believe to be rightfully ours.

Young Love Longings

i look to the sky as i did at nineteen
at thirty-nine it does not look the same

i still hope for you to come back to me
or someone like you who would love me

i hope i forget not
how to love
   — as i wait for love

wrinkles and bulges
have lowered my expectations

many afternoons i sit and stare
at blue skies
   — almost any love would do

i am stuck at nineteen
my soul is a hostage
   — longing for my dream.

1969 Frozen in Time

my guess is they were born
between 1951 and 1954
> *– this couple that sat at a corner table*
> *in an espresso coffee shop*

as i look their way the year
could be 1969

her french beret partly covering long
naturally straight hair

501 levi jeans and collarless shirt
vest and sandals with socks

his long hair and a long beard
501 levi jeans and t-shirt

vest and sandals and socks
leather wrist bands

her silver peace symbol on a leather strap
around her neck

> *– icons of longing*
> *for a time that never came*

beliefs held in '69
the best they will ever have

so they hold true to their leanings
in attitude and dress

older now — yes — but i bet they only
see '69 in the mirror

as they sip their latte
press their cheeks together

laughing and sharing secrets the
way they did then

they catch me off guard as i watch
they stare back defiantly

i rub my hands over my eyes
        — reality check

i want them to do the same
        — reality check

but quickly and quietly they rise from the
table to whisk past me for the door

i watch them climb into an old van and
imagine them driving to
some forest campsite playing old '69 hits
sitting by a campfire
as we did that year before making our way
into the world

why is it some of us long for the past
to be the present

i would like to thank this couple for the memory
it was worth the time

the lady at the counter suddenly calls out
your latte is ready
abruptly bringing me back

> *— from that brief moment*
> *when i was frozen in time*
> *caught off guard by the*
> *forces of fado.*

Longing for Death

my love has passed and
i am without her

must i wait out life or can i
go to her now

would God punish such a love as
the love i have for her

if eternity begins
after we die
and if our peace
is complete
after we die
then come i to
my destiny

wait for me my love
i am on my way

if God does not
answer
whether i should
wait or go
i will
go

> *my longing cannot*
> *endure my loss.*

Loss and Time

1.
our eyes meet
and then
we look away

we were friends since nine
and then in one
argument it is gone

why can't we mend
did we
get too close

did our souls lose their
self-respect
in one argument.

2.
i miss the youthful years
of laughter

sharing secrets no one else
knew

how do we call
it back

how do we become again what we
were once to each other

do you even remember
do you care as i

sometimes i dream you call
and want me back

years have passed and i cannot
let these memories go

have you thought of me
since that day

when we lost it all.

> 3.
> *why do we feel differently*
> *when the clouds are out*
> *than*
> *when the*
> *sun*
> *is out*
>
> *— whatever the*
> *answer*
>
> *i know i would feel differently*
> *with you as my friend*
> *than not.*

> 4.
we trampled on
each other's
most precious
part
that which
doubts
the other's
trust

why did we not know this
and how to mend.

    5.
i freeze when i
see you

this loss forever unresolved

perhaps more time and life will
help me see loss otherwise

but for now i freeze
when i see
you.

Lost Light

1.
when my world went dark
i could see no way out
    — to live was hell
    to take my
    life would also
    be hell

crowded around my soul
indecision whether to
abandon taught answers
as to why i should live

or take the risk and
free myself of my
torment
    — depression is like this
    unable to live
    or die.

2.
years have passed
i live unable to risk the taught answers
while God offers none
for my torment

i trudge on until death comes at its own time
i dare not beckon it myself
again
    — death must find me now
    i am a failed suicide
    a lost light.

Nonwalking

i roll here
i roll there

i look up at the world
the world looks down
upon me

i dream of miles and miles of
trees and me running
in their midst

my waking hours are sad
most of all

>*peace comes only
>in my dreams*

occasionally i get lost in a
movie or a book

sometimes i can sit with friends
and enjoy their stories

i can laugh with them yet
inside i cry

>*if only to stand and walk
>it is all i ask.*

Seize Me Not

1.
seize me not

take another route
through me

seize me not

change course and travel
not the known road

seize me not

find a path through
the brain maze.

2.
electricity charges
along the paths of
my nerves

what are the odds
of a failure of the
right signals

no answer

live with it they say
or take these pills.

3.
so i have learned to
live with it
    — the occasional seizure

thus far no real damage
but what are the odds
that one day this path
in my brain seizes
up completely

or that it opens up
and never bothers
me again.

Peace in Guilt

no turning back the
crime is done

i run until i am out of breath but
keep moving nonetheless

the scene plays over and over
wrath like a poison to my soul

why could i not have let her leave
let her find what i could not give and did not have

jealousy sought its own reward
leaving me to clean up the evidence

> *where is resolve for me now*
> *do i confess and live my*
> *life confined*
>
> *or do i stay in the shadows*
> *forever on the*
> *run*
>
> *confession – will you*
> *free my soul*

i cannot know until i walk through
that door so until then i will
travel by way of shadows

i cannot call death back
and am unwilling to
give myself to her

*— so i search for a peace
within my guilt.*

The Other Side (1)

1.
flowers in
bloom

sun is out
sky is blue

though my window
has views

i am lonely still.

2.
fear of failing in friendship
has brought me here
alone

my solitude safe enough
as i watch myself
erode

content allowing age to come to me this way
rather than risk failing again
in friendship.

3.
gaunt and frail
fat and lazy

though i bathe and scrub
the dirt stays

i wish this upon
no one

days are long and
years swift

having lost at life
i still breathe.

    4.
all i would have to do is
rise and venture out

tell someone good day
enjoy the outing

but solitude has gotten
the best of me.

    5.
hooked on solitude
i cannot let her go

i hate her
yet i cling to her

stroking my aching soul with kindness
she taunts me mocks me
says to me

you did not see my other side
so who's to blame.

6.

where is the safety in solitude
where is the danger
where is the line

how many souls have faced defeat
when they seek only to retreat

> *— my soul has fallen into this abyss*
> *and it cannot climb out.*

The Other Side (2)

i reach for your hand
there is none there

years have passed
the love we had was
the best of life

i haunt the places
we used to go

i am as a ghost to myself
as i sip our favorite wine
in our favorite café

i close my eyes
go back in time

i see me dying ever so slowly
embers of my life
turning dim

who writes the rules of morality
and who decides

    evidently it is we

i cannot call back my lust
for a stranger that one night

if my soul chooses death
the raison d'etre

i journey there by choice

if i wait for you to forgive
i risk that as well

do i wait and miss you
or do i choose my end now

> *God if i offend You*
> *i apologize*
>
> *but You have not come*
> *to me in my grief*
>
> *You did not save me*
> *from my lust*
>
> *so i ask now that You*
> *look the other way*
>
> *i am grotesque*
> *either alive or dead.*

Worshiping You ...

Confession of a sixteen-year-old

my worship is to watch you
worship

i remain inadequate before God without
watching you

    i am ugly next to you

your beauty allows my acceptability
before God

but when i am alone
God is not there

but next to you i feel
His presence

    i am fat i am ugly

    God looks away
    from me

i long for the day when
i need you not

and when God convinces me of
a beauty of my own.

The Valley of Religion and the Mountain of God

1.

i looked down upon the valley i needed to cross
in order to get to the mountain of God

there stood many cabins and
garden plots

with boundary lines
around them

signs and gates obvious
at every cabin

i would have to pass by them all
to get to the other side

why did the thought of crossing
this valley frighten me so

i could see the mountain on the other side
and that is where i wanted to go

i feared that i would be tempted to stay
in the valley if i dared try to cross it.

2.

i heard many stories of how others
had stopped in the valley
and never made it to the mountain
why would i be any different

years have passed
i never ventured into the valley
only watched it but never
tried to make my way to the mountain

this kind of safety has a sorrow that slowly starves one's soul
is it better to try and know one's make
or to languish in mystery and
long for what risk one
will never take.

Lesson 101 in Fado

hope is my call as i wait
i believe i am entitled

my wants and needs
give meaning to my life

i would rather drown in
hope than abandon my desires

brought to the edge and
left to fend for myself

i prefer to hope alone
rather than be surrounded by a crowd
of disappointed friends

fado is my love
fado is my pain
fado is my soul
fado are the eyes of my desire

right or wrong makes no sense
when i cannot be convinced

rational choice
an enemy to my hope

lead me to the edge
leave me to contemplate my dreams

longing is a better choice than
to abdicate hope and live only in certainty

fado is my love
fado is my pain
fado is my soul
fado are the eyes of my desire.

Fado One

this hour will last
me a lifetime
if we can
hold
each other
and share our
love
for one more
moment in
time

a cold wind presses
against our
cheeks
but i
only
think of yours
pressed
against
mine

there will be too
many love
poems
too many
lovers
who
aspire to
the same
but they could not
change this day

we must part
and hope
that fate can
bring us
back
here again

our fathers' love
of different
Gods separates us

    — as we embrace on this cold night
    allow me one more minute before
    my lover's warm breath
    is taken from me.

Fado Two

i miss me

i am rarely me
these days

i take long
walks and
imagine
if i
were not
me
what
would
i be doing
now

i am
fading
as is the
memory
of who
i am

i lost a
child to
leukemia
he was
a darling

i am what
you would
call lost
in fado

having my child back in my arms
is the only healing acceptable
i dream of him often
my dreams are my only peace

leukemia like lightening
struck him down
i will fade now into darkness
and dream
so the light of my longing
can shine on him.

Children

1.
no child
. . . barren

never experienced
. . . birth

no answer to
. . . prayer

no meaning of
. . . children

no God for
. . . miracle

no virtue in
. . . waiting.

2.
if i cannot conceive
what meaning do i have
in life

if i could call back my own
birth i would be
unborn

i walk the longing path
of prayer

my smile is faint
my speech is quiet

is there a place of peace
where the barren
can scream.

A Thousand Souls

a thousand souls i see on this beach
souls like me who seek the sea
to swallow them rather than
live another day

no crime committed no injustice known
only loneliness and despair calling
them here

no poverty do they know nor despair of love
rather a place inside that
spits out life

depression for no reason
wounded living without peace
does God understand
does God care

> *how can i hold no grudge toward God*
> *when i believe God has the power*

a thousand souls i see
a thousand more have been
thousands more yet to come
all have thought this through

from the sands of the beach to the ocean
their choice of death — when the longing calls

> *death is the chosen peace*
> *for a thousand souls like me.*

And Then What

first drop of dew
i could taste it
sweet clean
and fresh

sunrise opened with
a spray of light
warm and
secure

two strong arms lifted me
formed the pillow just right
for me to see out the window
the morning sun my only comfort
against the enemy inside

morning colors wakening my delight
moments of joy shutting out the
pain inside from this slow
decaying nerve
disease

as always
this moment slipped by
—it is not fair

i cannot make the joy
last more than a moment before
my disease intrudes

the great *why me* goes unanswered
if you were in my stead it would
be as critical to you as it is
to me

a sunrise no matter how magnificent
cannot cure for long the
stench of my
body

colors array the sky
i smile with tears
and laugh with
sadness

 – if i pray to God it is only because
all other hope has left me.

Dead Butterflies

1.

cotton shirts are cool
in the sun and warm
in the shade
trading kisses in the
afternoon with you is
the best way to love.

2.

when i see a butterfly
in flight my eyes
light up

a dead butterfly makes
me wonder
why

simple are my joys in life
complex are my unknowns
in death

how does the life of a butterfly and
cotton shirts and sun and shade
and trading kisses with you
bring me here where i
must write about it
this way.

3.
i like least the part about the dead butterfly
it reminds me of my own mortality
and my brief time on earth

my kisses with you are my prize.

Hu-man Longings One

1.

water water
life to my lips
life to my throat
i walk miles and miles
for water

meat meat
i must eat
my stomach desires meat
day and night i search
for a kill to eat

shade for my head
shelter from rain
fire at night
warms the cold
i want a place where
i can rest my soul

i gather around with
others like me
we are safety in the many
mating for
reasons not easily
remembered.

2.
i am hu-man
master of earth

i am hu-man
slave to a power
not known

i long to know
who and what is
the meaning
of me

meanwhile it is —
water water
meat meat

shade shelter
fire sleep
safety
and mate.

Hu-man Longings Two

1.

i have spears
i have shelter
i have water
i have a companion
i have children

but my soul is restless
for unseen is a power
that calls upon me
day and night
    — then hides itself
    and though i search
    i never
    find it

spears
shelter
water
companion
children
do not fill the void
from this voice
that calls.

2.

i am hu-man
both of God
and earth

i wrestle with
a mystery
that steals
from me
both my God
and my earth

answers to this unknown
are like rain falling into the ocean
— how do we count the drops
how do we separate them from
where they fall.

Hu-man Longings Three

i long for a land of my own
where my name is my land
where my identity is of the earth

i long for a land where my hand recognizes the soil
how can i explain to my children that i can give them my name
but no land

though i laugh and i smile and enjoy good days
the land i work is a land that belongs to another

my spirit worries not it has a home of its own
but i cannot shun my own worry for an earthly land
despite my belief that our spirits live on

why is my peace not content with my spirit alone

i long for a land of my own
where my name is my land
where my identity is of the earth

for i am of both — earth and spirit.

Found Diary Page

i
have thoughts
of my own

i
have plans of
my own

i
am equal to
the male

i
know how to make
him complete

i
am kept silent
all day long
by him

i
am kept as
a servant
by him

i
am kept as a prisoner
by him
that i might not run

so i
hide my diary
from my husband

in my world i roam in a male pasture
with one bull and many cows

all the years have passed all the love
i had for my mate as milk for calves

i could tell him of all the love he missed
but now he too is out to pasture so why waste
breath on memories that cannot revive life.

Immigrant One

1.
pick the crop
make the bed
wash the dishes
do not sleep till i am fed

what kind of immigrant do we want
the kind who is free like us
or who we keep down forever

there is a noise in my head
i refuse to hear

there is a gnaw at my heart
i refuse to give

there is a choke-hold on my spirit
i refuse to admit

my soul goes cold when the fire
of my indignation spews righteousness

as my greed grows i am dying
and my life starves from within

my selfish want imprisons
all rational compassion

pick the crop
make the bed
wash the dishes
do not sleep till i am fed

we are like many other nations in history
that believe that because we rule
our freedom is a virtue and that others
who want it but do not have it
are simply inferior.

2.

i pricked my finger on a thorn
and screamed for help

you fell and were crippled
i saw you not because
of the prick on my finger

but a faint voice i heard like
a chorus in my head
pounding like a hammer
to a nail

no immigrant shall
sleep till all the pricks
on my finger are attended

i am a doomed self-righteous life
void of consciousness that will not
give up my own comfort
for the life of another

pick the crop
make the bed
wash the dishes
do not sleep till i am fed.

Immigrant Two

1.
out loud i say —
>   *go home*
>   *i want you not*
>   *you are not american*

aside i whisper —
>   *come*
>   *in the night*
>   *come in the back way*
>   *to my home*
>   *for i have need of you*
>   *to carry my load.*

2.
in the light i speak lies
but at night i seek you
in the dark

i beckon you with food
but give you warning
not to be seen with me in the day

on my mirror i have pasted these words —
>   *an immigrant is a person who is not a*
>   *person with rights or privileges*
>   *why must i feel guilty over*
>   *immigrants*

though no words are actually pasted there
they exist
for my actions have written them and placed
them there.

Part Three: The Priest in Us

Introduction

we are the priests of our lives

all others are those
who parade as
having spiritual authority
over us

i choose not to
give my priesthood
away.

Guides

theologies
doctrines
beliefs
fall
short
— they prove not
their God
is without flaw

therefore is it not
reasonable to suggest
that our own
failure is
between us
and our
God
— i hold
no one
responsible

perhaps
we are each
meant to be
the priest
of our own
lives
— where no priest
other than we
are held accountable for
our failures

as far as
seeking God
in our own way
perhaps
we are spiritual travelers
meant to draw our own maps
as we go
— where no one
has this authority over us
it is our map
to draw.

Priest One

1.
hu-man
look
within
therein
lies a
priest

one
spirit
born
to
one
body

rich
or
poor
lost
or
found
none
are
rejected
by
God

all
are priests
all
are equal
all
are accepted

allow
the priest
in you
to rise
up.

2.
God
covenant-maker
with all spirits

can we walk
as You
made
us to walk

can we
expel
the people
from our-
selves
who want
to reign
over our
priest-
hood

i look only
to You
God
as my
guide

and therefore
acknowledge

my
priest-
hood
and You.

Priest Two

1.

there is day
there is night
there is earth
there is rain
– under God's sky

i feel alone
surrounded
by all the living
from start to finish
i am the selfish
who seeks control

how could i have
destroyed so
quickly what was given
so freely.

2.

there is day
there is night
there is earth
there is rain
– if there is life is there God

does the day and the night
and the earth and the rain
and all life have rights
equal to my own

i am but one
of many priests
who live here

and of the souls not human
do they also have spirits
are they also created to be
priests over their lives

— there is no limit or boundary here
it is only i who thought there was.

Priest Three

what if salvation is not tomorrow's reward
what if salvation is here today if
we keep within our sights the difference
between arrogant intolerance and the value
of all human life as equal to our own.

I Believe

i believe if jesus had lived longer
his beliefs would have evolved and changed

i cannot prove this
but feel it is more likely than not

for our beliefs
are all products of
evolution and change.

How to Clear One's Head

clouds are rolling in from the south

my head is foggy

i hear music and voices faintly from a distance

the wind is howling

days like this cause me to feel aimless

— what is life all about

if i shut myself in confusion builds

like a storm

if i should seek from whence the voices and music come

and dare fail at the art of the social graces

dare watch others mingle and enjoy life

dare to observe and engage

will my own comfort

be satisified

the clouds and wind are rolling in

a permanent ache from within pounds

pounds against my loneliness

seeking my demise by

causing me to regress

and spend my days shut in

how is it that i isolate myself from my longing

to enjoy a social gathering

— it is all i want —

but instead i hide in dark rooms

fearing the chatter of a crowd

how is it that what i want waits in sunny days and interaction

but am paralyzed with fear

at the thought of going outside

into the warmth and the sight of people

how is it that a knocking at my door

finds me both relieved and afraid

debating with myself whether or not

to answer

i fear i am alone here and that no one hears

a victim hiding within his own thoughts

i am too deep in a hole to dig myself out

i need someone who can lift me

but no one can be seen on the horizon

for my doors are locked and the lights dim

let this be a message for any who see such lonely beings

who may only be waiting for a tap on the shoulder

to shore them up

the safety of solitude can become a cruel cruel beast.

His Funeral Is Tomorrow

the windows were caked with dirt
for the windstorm blew hard
and dust swirled till it
became dirt

the moisture in the air turned
the dirt into a mud-cake batter
and the wind spun it
everywhere

the loneliness of my friend
who had returned from
iraq was full of
memories of
iraqi dirt

his insides in despair
a silent rage caused his
outsides to whirl
like an iraqi
storm

he knew he could
not stay
here

once having lived
a soldier's life
it is hard to
leave it

there is peace in my soul as a soldier
unless you have experienced war
like this you can never
know what it is i am saying

that was the last time
i heard his voice

his funeral is
tomorrow.

The Value of You

through my eyes
my soul
sees the value
of *you*

we are alike
you and i
on this earth
ride

we both have
a soul and
a spirit and a desire
for life

we both need air
to breathe
and food to eat

cannot we coexist
valuing ourselves
as equals.

I Will Call it Heaven

to imagine life without burden
is like imagining a place
where no one has to
carry the weight of
his humanity
any longer

i will call that place heaven

— *imagine that.*

Wednesday Afternoon Coffee and Cotton Farming

occasionally my grandfather would shut off the tractor
and go to town for a wednesday afternoon coffee
where farmers would meet to discuss their crops

it seems this was an agreement made
among many of the cotton farmers of his
small southwestern texas community

as the story goes at one of these coffee sessions
a younger farmer asked my grandfather why he came

as his crop was always well-groomed
and yielded more cotton than any other
of the farmers around

my grandfather explained that if what the young man
said was true it was because my grandfather
came to listen learn and contribute his view

he said
one man cannot know all there to know about cotton farming

once at a bible study coffee session i shared this story
with a few men who insisted they knew all about God
and what God requires us to do.

Thoughts That Remain

Excerpts of an unfinished poem from my youth

i saw myself in a dream —

an old man
sitting under a shade tree
writing these words

i once ran up and down hills
the muscles of my youth
playing till dawn became dusk

but now i think more and sit more
my age does not stir me
to run the hills anymore

sleep comes when night is early
there is a way that leads to life
— where the fire refines the silver
and grass withers in the sun

are we mortal
and immortal
simultaneously.

What Am I to Think

1.

what was i to think
when a group of conservative evangelical christians i know
made these comments the week after easter

islam is evil and we have a God-given right
to protect our freedom
we are to rule
we are not to be servants to islam
rather it is to be servant to us.

2.

what am i to think
when the conservative evangelical christian speakers
wear the best clothing and have the best seats and collect money
for themselves in the name of God

what am i to think
what gospel is this they preach

it is not the gospel of the bible i read.

Wise Notes from an Elder

1.
wisdom given where i have
not tread has not the depth
i imagine it does.

2.
rushing to be wise should
be clue enough of its
wisdom.

3.
wisdom without time and
struggle as its foundation
is not reliable wisdom.

4.
being wise before any gray
shows in the hair
is the same as taking bread
out of the oven before
its time.

Mountaintop Ministry

top of a mountain
at the ridge
the wind blew
strong across my path

the horizon melted
into the sky

i had climbed
this mountain before
and nearly fallen
but today the climb gave me
a sensation of freedom
i had learned how
to climb
i had not given up

and with each step
i had learned
to ask

— *what next.*

Surrender

my commune with
my God is
clear

no pew of wood
no cross of gold
no rituals
dressed
in silk

in solitude i
worship

i surrender here
to my soul's
unique
self.

Lost Excerpts

root of my soul
depth of my being
lives a human
and a god

plow and harvest
winter-wise
shelter and rules
earthly gruel

sacrifice to gods
and humans alike
voids are filled
til called are we to die

history teaches
us naught
earth is mystery still
we her guardian
tilling her soil
stealing her life

years pass and
still no answer
can we agree
why we
are here

our final epitaph to read—
on our own
without a
map.

Two Gods Cannot Occupy the Same Soul

my secret
for years
was that
i was not
a christian
although
i was
christian

deep inside
i believed
jesus was
no deity
and hell
was only fear
without
answers

i struggle not
alone here
i see others
yawn in the
pew
peek at their
watches

hours
of sermons
like
cartoons
without
the fun

pseudo have i
lived in the
rooms of
christian
faith

but the day
i walked
away
i saw
clearly

two Gods
cannot
occupy
the same
soul.

I Dream of God

does God live
in a place where
only our spirits
are allowed
to go

in our sleep do
our spirits awake
to commune
with God

body
mind
soul
take your
rest now
while
my spirit
communes with
God

i wonder —
is this
just another
of the many paths
to the unseen
God.

Silent Places

where God speaks
there are no words

where God is
no voice is heard

the silent places
of my soul
search for You there

is the message
getting through.

Sleepy Eyes

sleepy eyes shut the world out
wake my spirit so i can
know where you roam
in the dark hours of night

through crowded thoughts i push
my way into my spirit
not to miss one minute
of celestial travel

spirit let me in so i can learn of
your comings and your goings
wake me when the time comes
for me to take my bow

sleepy eyes shut the world out
let dreams take me where
my spirit worships

there will i take my rest

what better venture than
going where our spirit goes.

Inner Contemplation

though i seem quiet
inside i am not

though i conform
i rest not

though i look content
i am in conflict

though i seek faith
i have doubt

though i am free to go
my soul is trapped

one day i begin to wake
and see my life in waste

i let go of that which
causes me grief

i put the cross in a drawer
and wear it no more

gradually i become the me
i was made to be

now God has come to life in a
form i can believe

the sun is more pleasant
the breeze more comforting

the day has more promise
God is more real

it is a wise saying still
— seek God while He may be found.

Where Goes My Prayer

1.
where goes my prayer
does it evaporate into thin air

or is it like a shot in the dark
where there is no target no mark

are there truths we will never know

why is it what we believe to be true today
may not be true tomorrow.

2.
if there is a boundary for humans
i believe the evidence is in

that it says yes
because we've dug our own abyss

we are earth's only enemies
she has allowed us so much leniency

we are the worst of creation
fighting amongst ourselves for reasons undefined

if this is who we are
i must forsake prayer and prepare for war.

3.

to want to change what God has not nor ever will
is this the fate to which i fear i am bound

what will compel us to seek a vision better than
the one that seeks only a God who agrees with us

the God i see comes not to save or destroy
but to watch from the heavens

and that is enough for me to want
to value ourselves and the earth
believing earth is His gift

the rest is up to us
will we raze or we will save.

A Thought on Good and Evil

inner depths
speak to my deep
parts

shallow parts
be not satisfied with what you
have found

evil hearts
come to gain while
compassionate hearts
come to aid

words
no matter how true
do not persuade evil
away

*— we live
what we believe.*

Equal

i know a man eighty-four years old who is an atheist
fairly compassionate honest who treats people as equals

i know a christian who says only God can create
compassion honesty and a sense of equality
in people with the requirement that they believe
in the christian God

i ask if the atheist lives a compassionate life
without God does that make the christian wrong

does God work in us all regardless of the belief
with which we settle

if an atheist stands as an equal with those
who value life as equal to their own
then i am grateful to stand with him and
all others who believe the same.

Convenience Store Prophet

he is a construction contractor
a lean-built hispanic
with piercing yet friendly eyes
slightly graying hair shaven
though always with a few days' growth

strong in stature
rough hands that move gently
he seems at peace
though his pacing expresses otherwise

— this is the convenience store prophet

propped up against the counter
he sips his cup of coffee
with powdered cream and
white sugar in a styrofoam cup
at break time 10:00 a.m.

a flannel shirt torn in places
paint spills and oil spots here and there
pants that mirror the shirt

work boots that have seen plenty of winters
resoled and resoled again
a leather belt well-worn
and a cap with a wind-swept look
that has seen many washings

— this is the convenience store prophet

it's been maybe thirty-six years since i met him
back when he went door to door
passing out biblical literature

once i visited him at home and since then
we've continued the same long-running conversation

being this is a small town our paths cross often
when they do we take the time to talk
to converse about the end times
the subject we began more than three decades ago

more often than not he can be found about 10:00 a.m.
everyday or so at this same convenience store
sipping his coffee at break time

— this is the convenience store prophet

though we agree on little this is something
he does not know for i tend to agree with him
allowing him to voice his concerns about the world
and the answer he believes must come

though i find it strange that the end of time
has been playing out for thousands of years

his opinions can be harsh yet i know him to be gentle
always ready to help a stranded stranger
therefore to me regardless of his ramblings
the fact that he is truly kind makes him
the best kind of friend to have

— this is the convenience store prophet

i stop by every now and then to chat and
enjoy his friendship
he can always be found at the convenience store
which has become his sunday pulpit

i prod him on—he wants me to—so he can respond
because as far as he is concerned the end times
may arrive any moment
so he is always prepared to ask anyone passing by

are you ready.

Intro to Packin'

it was like seeing a UFO
it happened so quick
it caught me by
surprise

i have had to replay
the event over
and over

having said this however
it really did happen.

Packin'

I attended a meeting in March 2010 where a man referred to as Sheriff Mack spoke. When Sheriff Mack entered the room the audience was suddenly electrified with emotion. I think the first words out of his mouth were "Who's packin'?"

I learned then the meaning of that phrase.

Sheriff Mack opened his suit jacket to reveal his pistol and shoulder holster. I looked around; many others were standing up to show their pistols. Loud roars of approval came from most everyone who was there. Sheriff Mack then gave a short presentation on our right to bear arms and form state militias.

The reason for this presentation was to clarify that state governments had more legal rights and say on gun control than the federal government. Sheriff Mack implied that it was our God-given right to bear arms, and when he said that many hollered "Amen!"

I guess I shouldn't be alarmed by meetings like this, but my interest in this one in particular was because it was held at a local evangelical church. Why there? I guess I am naive as to the teaching of Jesus concerning our rights to bear arms and fight or sue anyone who denies us that right.

Sheriff Mack had won a lawsuit that went all the way to the Supreme Court concerning the states' sovereignty over certain gun control issues. But why did the meeting have to be at a church where the pastor offered prayer and God's guidance?

I could have been anywhere in any sanctuary of any religion . . .
The arrogance of such talk caused me to leave the meeting,
not trusting the attendees for they did not appear to be open to debate
or disagreement.

As I went about my day, after that evening meeting a song came to
me —

who's packin'
anyone who's anyone is packin'
we are the chosen of america
and blessed by God
who's packin'

anyone who knows freedom is packin'
we are freedom fighters for God
we have the God-given right
to bear arms
who's packin'

anyone who's for christ is packin'
gun-toting christianity is the
new word of God

packin', packin', packin',
wear it show it
packin' for all to
see

packin',
packin',
packin'

who's packin'.

Zombie

i always thought it would be fun
just once to be made up
like one of those zombies
in the movies and do
a scene

until one day i saw a real live
zombie — at which point
i saw nothing enter-
taining in it
at all

the zombie has a name
crack methamphetamine.

Rambling Prophet

bronze sunrise
full clouds
glistening light
against morning
dew and
me standing
next to the
edge of a mountain
cliff

all seemed right
except above
me perched
in a tree was a raven
as white as white
could be

i was startled to
see that above
my head its
claws
sat barely
six feet away

why was the raven there
so quiet and so still
as if it
were enjoying the
sunrise
as i

the raven inched
over closer
to me
suddenly landing
at my feet
a reptile
in its grasp

then away he went

i imagined it a
spiritual moment
but most likely
the raven had only
breakfast on his
mind

so
what else spiritually
might i have
wrong

the rest of day i was daunted
by the thought that
my spiritual beliefs were
standing on the edge
of absurdity

yet it seems the edges are
where revelations dwell
and mysteries unravel

　　　— along with ravens
　　　looking for breakfast.

Persecutors

the ones who have power over others
are always the persecutors

religiously speaking
none are innocent here.

A Victory

a victory
is when my soul
argues less
with those
with whom it
disagrees.

Feed the Poor or Save the Cross

as a group of young christians walked
through a meadow where
youth rallies were held
they noticed a ten-foot-tall cross
lying on the ground

some of the group were outraged
and so stayed there to lift the cross
back up to where it had been
while the rest of the group decided
it would not do to miss their appointment
volunteering at the soup kitchen
and so would fill in for the others
who'd stay behind

when the ones who stayed behind to lift up
the cross arrived they defended their
decision to be late as if re-erecting the cross
were a virtuous act of more value than
working in the soup kitchen

the ones who had not stayed to help with the cross
tried to ignore the comments of those who'd stayed
and continuing their task until the soup was gone

it is well to note here that the ones who'd left
the fallen cross considered their commitment
to the soup kitchen of more value than being late
in order to re-erect a cross in a meadow

thus it is – young christians learning how to divide.

Youth and Their Horses

i live in a small town with a small university
in the foothills of the southwestern mountains
of new mexico

our town attracts young people of all kinds
because of its size the university
and the national forest

sitting in an espresso coffee house listening
to a group of young people's chatter
my thoughts carried me to record the event
in this way

natural
healthy
wanting life
wanting
time to live

no flash
all function
wearing used
ignoring
the new

jeans
sandals
socks or
no socks
braids and
no makeup

lean
no extra fat
interesting
with smiles
and far-away
looks

engaging
articulate
leaning
toward
each other
for effect

what
will they
become as
years pass

i was there
once
so were
all my
friends

change
came
we
found out
choices
carry
consequences

the horse
youth rides
has no
reins

i know
the scars
from
riding those
horses.

The Grackle and the Cat

the cat strolled by the grackle
about twenty feet away

the grackle flew upward about
eight feet then landed
behind the cat

and began to hop behind it

the cat stopped and turned around
and jumped at the grackle

the grackle flew upwards another eight feet

the cat continued to stroll and
the grackle again began to
follow behind the cat
about ten feet away

they repeated their strategy at least six times

i wondered — were they both having fun
or was the grackle teasing the cat
or was something else happening
of which i was not aware

the lives of grackles and cats are not
like ours though we imagine them
from time to time to have human
attributes

*i enjoyed their performance
whatever their motive.*

Youth Denied

being denied
her youth
at fifty-two
she sought
it again
to complete
what she believed
she'd missed

thirty pounds
overweight
flesh in wrinkles
with two boys
reared and
gone

now she has
become
the girl
she warned
her boys
about

tight jeans
fat crowded in
nowhere
to go

though days
pass quickly
she will not
give up
her quest
for youth

to be denied
one's youth
is a hard lesson
to accept

youth unlived
is like a gap in
the memory
without a
map

her desire to fit
into tight jeans
is the
direction
her map
leads

— has she chosen a longer route
because of her need for
tight-fitting jeans.

Medicare Plan Part D Day

three elderly hispanic women
waited their turn to enroll in the
medicare plan part d

i was there on behalf of my mother-in-law

the forms and instructions a maze of
choices most likely designed by
a college tech graduate

in no way did the presentation make
sense to anyone over twenty

so while we waited for a counselor
i observed these three elderly women

one was quiet and only spoke when she
had to using as few words as possible

one was so loquacious that every second of
every minute of every hour of every
waking moment of the day
i swear she must talk
non-stop

and one contributed to the conversation
with ease and common sense
listening and understanding how to
add to the subject
at hand

though each different in personality
they all had a beauty in their eyes
and countenance

my guess is they were from several generations
of catholics and therefore it seemed to me
that confession and the virgin mary had
worked for them

their bearing seemed to say we have
absorbed all that is good in our faith

i was touched deeply by these women that day

   — *i saw within them the real priests of their lives.*

A Fear and a Peace . . . Garbled in a poem

one of my fears is also my peace
— that i am not satisfied with my answer
about what happens to us after we die

on one hand i am relieved to have freedom
to form my views unimpeded
by unacceptable answers

on the other the unresolved mystery
gnaws at me because maybe this is one
mystery we should know how to solve

afterall
is a sense of inner peace concerning one's belief
proof of its truth or is a fear of one's belief
proof of its truth

whichever
am i safe then if i have both a fear and a peace
concerning my belief that we have no answers

i admit
a sense of humor concerning it all helps my peace find
root in me despite the mystery and helps my
fear take a backseat.

Gretchen's Shaman

1.

the first time i saw the image of gretchen's shaman she was digging in
the earth for herbs

her hair was long and tied back and she was healthy and the freshly
dug earth was on her face hands and arms

her look was determined as she busied herself
with her "mission"

i interrupted her work and she peered at me with a look
that said "whatever you want it had better be good because
you are interrupting me"

though she spoke without malice or anger
serious and willing to set down her chore she queries me
with her eyes if i am in need.

2.

the second time i saw gretchen's shaman was in a dream
sitting on a log in the forest looking down a path
her hair untied and the breeze gently moving it about

she was contemplative and seeking an answer concerning the path
of the future and though she could not determine the future
she was becoming confident in her contemplation
for she could see that she had been preparing for
these days for some time and that she could
walk this path without having
to know the future
or being anxious
about it

she was wearing what appeared to be a nightgown
the time was late in the evening as the sun was setting

she had the appearance of being carved by the earth
and formed by the spirit

she walked as being of both earth and spirit

she was prepared to meet what lay ahead
without having to know what it was

her past was her strength
her peace to go forward

i saw memories of someone's mother pass by my dream
without knowing for sure i believe it was gretchen's
memory of her mother

perhaps the shaman brought the memory to gretchen as a reminder
that she has the strength to face the future
without knowing where the path leads.

The Newme Poem

i have nothing
but
what is in this house
it is all paid
in full

it may not appear
as much
but i have
no debt

and because i have
none
my faith is a lighter
burden.

Late Summer

it is late summer in the gila forest
river banks are
full of color

blues yellows whites and
reds are blooming
everywhere

wood lilies lavender thistles
gila rose and indian
paintbrush scatter
their scent

the gila river is running strong
and the breeze gives us
clues that autumn
is near

i watch my wife bend on one knee
and dip her hand in the river
she says it is cold
and i smile

i do not have the words to describe
my joy at being with my wife
here in the gila
by the river

i am full with life i am still

this moment will pass and i will
only have my memory of this day to
bring back the smile i have at this moment

— today is my birthday.

Prelude for Lyvonne

i watched a very close friend pass away
one of the spiritual travelers at their best

she entered the next realm with a most
profound dignity

she was learning to die on her own that day
the priest in her rose and ministered to my soul.

Lyvonne's Death . . . Three hours before

my friend the breeze
holds me gently
i am safe

my companion the sky
is with me always
a shield against
loneliness

my heart the forest trees
minister to me the
unknown of
tomorrow

where would i be
without my sunday hike

memories lead me
along this trail

it is my last
hike here

i see the crest of
the hill

beyond the crest
i cannot see

where would i be
without my sunday hike

i am at peace for my memories
carry me to the
crest

my fate
leads me to tomorrow's trail
eternity is my calm
my breeze
my companion
my forest
trees

where would i be
without my sunday hike.

Lyvonne Learning to Die

1.
i watched a friend
die today

she was sixty-nine
and healthy

or so she
thought

diagnosed with stage iv
multiple myeloma

she was breathing
steady

breathing
hard

her eyes were closed
ignoring us

she was involved in a more
urgent matter

— she was busy dying.

2.
she said to us a few
days prior

if i cannot have the quality
of life i want

then i do not want
to live

a sick and slow
death

— i want to go quick.

    3.
i watched her allow peace
to embrace her

breathing steady
breathing hard

— then a sudden change.

    4.
i saw the life leave her
though she breathed
for two more
hours

she was not here anymore
all that remained was
her breath

i learned how to die today
from my friend

— thank you.

A Friend's Discovery of God

This is the story of how a middle-aged man with a wife and children was struck down suddenly by a bone disease. What I saw was the priest in him coming alive. No one could answer for him or map out his path.
No one was there to show him when it was time to pass on — that was his decision to make and only his. This poem is from a dream I had about him and the words he spoke to me.

i had not planned on learning
of God and of my spirit
with bone disease
as my guide

but i am now closer to God
and my spirit be-
cause of the
disease

i fell one day fixing a fence
and since then life has
not been the
same

my family suffers grief more than i
  — i am ready

though i would not miss my life
my family says
it is better if
i stay

giving up what could have been
giving up well-laid plans for
this bed is not the

way i wanted
to know
God

the closeness i feel to God is indescribable
the emptiness is as indescribable
but this is the God i know
and the life i
have

few bodily functions and
a daily toil of pain
all this just
to know
God

come peace
come death
take me

but give my
family the life
they want

protect them from
knowing You as
i have had to
know You

give them the joy of life
and show them how
not to grieve long

and give me the wisdom
to know when to say
enough

– i am ready.

About the Author

Tony Prewit was born in Stamford, Texas in 1954 and then moved with his family at the age of eight to Silver City, New Mexico. He has earned both bachelor's and master's of arts degrees and has traveled extensively throughout the United States as a musician. Besides his interest in poetry, the author has written, directed, and performed in several plays and as a mime actor. In addition, he is an artist who delves in photography, charcoals, pastels, and watercolors. Art is his private therapy.

For over thirty-five years the author kept a journal of poetry that chronicled his most secret, inner struggles with his belief in God. During that time he lived what seemed to be a fairly normal life — traveling, going to school, marrying, and owning a retail furniture company. This journal, however, does not chronicle his "normal" life, but his struggles with belief. He believes many people have these same kinds of inner challenges with life, and this journal brings to the forefront the reality of these challenges.

Since 1978 he has lived with his wife Pat, a classical pianist, in Silver City, New Mexico, the place he considers home for its culture, land, seasons, and people.

Made in the USA
San Bernardino, CA
06 January 2019